Frenzy of Color, Reverie of Line

Poems on Vincent van Gogh's Life and Art

by
Lenny Lianne

Published by
ScriptWorks Press, 2010

2017 Edition by WordsonPage, an
Imprint of WordsonStage.net

Frenzy of Color, Reverie of Line:
Poems on Vincent van Gogh's Life and Art

© Copyright, Lenny Lianne, 2009
All Rights Reserved, Second edition Published
By WordsonPage, an imprint of WordsonStage.net

Manufactured in the United States of America
Editors: J. Douglas, K. McBlair
Cover Designer: Jean Klein
Cover Art: Fritillaries in a Copper Vase;
Vincent van Gogh; Summer 1887;
Dover Publications, Inc.

Library of Congress Cataloging in Publication Data
Printed in the United States of America

© Copyright, Lenny Lianne, 2009

Copyright Caution

Any public performance of *Frenzy of Color, Reverie of Line:* Poems on Vincent van Gogh's Life and Art is subject to payment of a royalty unless written permission is given waiving such fee. Except for brief quotations in critical reviews, this work may not be reproduced by any means. The Work is fully protected under the copyright laws of the United States of America, and of all countries covered by the International Copyright Union (including the Dominion of Canada and the rest of the British Commonwealth), and of all countries covered by the Pan-American Copyright Convention, the Universal Copyright Convention, and the Berne Convention, and of all countries with which the United States has reciprocal copyright relations. All rights, including public reading, radio broadcasting, television, video or sound recording, all other forms of mechanical or electronic reproduction, such as CD-ROM, CD-I, DVD, information storage and retrieval systems and photo-copying, and the rights of translation into foreign languages, are strictly reserved.

Grateful acknowledgement is made to the editors of the following publications in which these works appeared:

IODINE POETRY JOURNAL: "In the Arena"
MAGEE PARK POETS ANTHOLOGY: "In Arles"
SAN DIEGO POETRY ANNUAL: "The Presence"
TIDEPOOLS: "The Blunt Grace of Sunlight"

Grateful acknowledgement for the Van Gogh reproductions is made to Dover Publications, Inc., *Van Gogh's Paintings & Drawings, CD-ROM & BOOK*

A list of the museums in which the paintings are found begins on page 105

NOTE:

      In order to differentiate between the spoken words of Vincent van Gogh and other dialogue, I have italicized quotations from van Gogh and placed other imagined speech in quotation marks.

CONTENTS

A PRESENCE 9

DIGGER...13

ROAD IN ETTEN............................17

SORROW......................................21

ARTIST'S SIGNATURE....................27

GORDINA DE GROOT 31

STILL LIFES..................................35

THE BLUNT GRACE OF SUNLIGHT 39

SOMETHING ABOUT BRIDGES............43

IN ARLES 47

RACHEL OF ARLES.........................51

IN THE ARENA..............................55

MALICE..59

VAN GOGH'S HATS 63

IRISES 69

THE DEATH'S HEAD MOTH 73

CYPRESS TREES............................77

STARRY NIGHT 81

PAINTING THE STARS 85

BRANCH OF AN ALMOND TREE 89

ROAD WITH CYPRESS AND STAR........93

AT LAST 97

JULY 1890....................................101

Self-Portrait in Front of the Easel
Painting, oil on canvas
Paris, January 1888
Van Gogh Museum
Amsterdam

Vincent van Gogh

March 30, 1853 — July 29, 1890

8

A Presence

Peasant with Sickle, Seen from the Back
drawing; black chalk
Nuenen: August 1885
Kröller-Müller Museum,
Netherlands

A PRESENCE

In the Brabant, a borderland
of marshes and small farms,
the peasants spoke in low tones

about the pastor's boy, born
to the exact day, a year after
the first stillbirth

and given the same name
as if the parents had prayed
to make their ache incarnate.

As the boy grew, he absorbed
the strange gazes, the stares
and almost-hushed murmurs

how Death remained
always behind him,
attached to his past.

In his haste to escape,
he slouched off on his own,
across fields and into forests.

Picking up empty birds' nests,
water beetles lying barely alive
and soon-wilted wildflowers,

he discerned how Death
shambled, not behind him,
but always slightly ahead.

When he glanced at farm hands
scything rye grass in arcs,
wide as Death's lecherous smile,

he sensed snickering Death
was a ceaseless presence,
as sanguine as time.

In odd moments, as he outgrew
the village, he learned his life
endured as a borderland

between two gates, waiting
for him to grasp Death
as part pleasure, part pain.

Digger

Digger
Watercolor: charcoal,
heightened with white
Etten: September, 1881
Kröller-Müller Museum, Otterlo, The Netherlands

DIGGER
September, 1881

So much of country life nurtures
a need in me to, through art,
extol every aspect of nature.

Taking up my stub of charcoal,
which itself comes from the earth,
I practice putting down lines

that turn into a total picture. I want
my lines to produce form, the way
soil and seed bloom into food.

I've persuaded Piet Kaufman,
the gardener, to pose holding
a spade. He stands stiff as a plow

but, at least, lets me draw him
in patched shirt and pants
and not in his Sunday best.

Most of the other folks around here
remain adamant about posing
in clothes more suited for courting.

They consider being captured
on paper in common farm clothes
beneath their well-dressed dignity.

They can't grasp how I prefer
to paint the broken-soled boots
of plowmen, reapers and gleaners,

the worn-out shoes and wooden
clogs of those who've tended
the haystack, the heifer and hen.

I'm humbled by this simple country
living, with its striving and strength.
Let me try to portray this with grace.

Road in Etten

Road in Etten
Drawing: pencil, washed
Etten: October, 1881
The Metropolitan Museum of Art,
New York

ROAD IN ETTEN
Etten, 1881

The road doesn't say good-bye
but stays mute and moves on,
disappearing into a tenuous distance.

Our old village holds back so much,
even cutting top branches down
to bare-boned trunks, stunting
the willows that line the road.

These whittled-down trees resemble
so many hands reaching out,
not to pray – as the heavens appear
unconcerned – but to seek alms.

Perhaps it's time to turn my back
on my father – the village minister –
and his nearsighted faith. What good
is prayer when poor men starve?

Week after week much of me hungers
for more. From the grudging village,
the road promises a boundless world.

20

Sorrow

Bent Figure of a Woman
Drawing: pencil, pen, brush, sepia, washed. The Hague: May - early in the month, 1882. Kröller-Müller Museum, Otterlo, The Netherlands

Bent Figure of a Woman Drawing: pencil, pen, brush, sepia, washed The Hague:
May - early 1882
Kröller-Müller Museum, Otterlo, The Netherlands

SORROW

When it rains for days, I think of Sien
seated in the dark merino dress, its ruffled
layers slanting in opaque sheets. I've drawn
her on a wooden chair, as companion pieces.

She holds her head in her left hand, leaning
into the burden that the bent arm supports.
Downturned lashes and her braided bun
coming undone seem to emit a lengthy sigh.

From the reverse direction, she reveals her face.
Its expression, full of dejection, echoes
through her hunched figure with enough
misery to make my heart sink.

●

I chanced upon her in a cheap wine shop
in back of the train station in late January.
I was in need of company and she was cold.
Out of the winter wind, following a drink,
she told me she took in laundry or cleaned

but was too weak for either so to earn her fare
she strolled the streets, *you understand how.*
Pregnant, abandoned like a nasty, tainted rag,
she looked half-starved. Here was hardship
in need of rescue, and I was ready.

●

I sketch Sien in her long, loose nightshift
as she sits on the floor near the old stove.
Her cigar burns between her fingers, ignored,
as she scowls at some inward place.

When she sits, she slouches, so the skin
of her bony face sags and her whole body
tumbles into its own sadness. In her silences,
she falls into a crevasse of hopelessness.

When Sien poses naked on a dead tree stump,
her head hangs into her folded arms and a dark
braid, in disarray, collapses down her knobby back.
Her breasts fall flaccid but the belly puffs out.

I compose out-in-the-open and inside versions
entitled *Sorrow*. In each, I strive to disclose
not the naked body but the spirit, bedraggled
and tarnished, as if discarded in a savage storm.

Sien with cigar Sitting on the Floor near Stove
Drawing: pencil, black chalk, pen, brush, sepia, heightened with white
The Hague: April – late in month, 1882
Kröller-Müller Museum, Otterlo, The Netherlands

Sorrow
Drawing, black chalk
The Hague: April 10, 1882
Walshall Museum and Art Gallery, Walshall, UK

Artist's Signature

A Pair of Boots
Painting, Oil on Canvas
Paris: early year 1887
The Baltimore Museum of Art
The Cone Collection
Baltimore, MD

Vincent

ARTIST'S SIGNATURE

I sign my work, simply inscribing
Vincent. Nothing else but my name
in round, roman letters like pebbles
placed in a row to edge a path.

No *van Gogh*.

as if I were walking far away
from my father and his unctuous
faith, far from art-dealer uncles,
purely vendors with dulled tastes.

I am <u>not</u> a van Gogh.

Merely *Vincent* in plain letters
like wet footprints impressed by work
boots and wooden clogs of a peasant,
coming in from fields and croplands.

Vincent, signed in modest print.

Gordina de Groot

The Potato Eaters
Painting, oil on canvas
Nuenen, The Netherlands: April, 1885
Van Gogh Museum, Amsterdam

GORDINA DE GROOT
"The Potato-Eaters"
oil on canvas
Nuenen, April, 1885

Her fork poised above, not touching,
the small potatoes on the platter,
she stares, somewhat stunned,

as if, in one protracted moment,
she surmises that the sound
she hears is not the brown owl

outside her parent's cottage.
In the darkened room, all are lost
in whatever consumes them.

While Mother pours the coffee
the artist gave them, Father takes
the first cup before she's finished.

A child, old enough to be ignored,
stands by the low, wooden table.
The chap in a peaked cap,

who perches on a ladder-back chair
beside the bonneted Gordina,
looks away from the food

as his fork spears a small potato.
No one speaks, but she hears
the meager query: "Who?"

Nothing long and lovely,
just the plain, one word
that frames the question,

and in its wake Gordina
is left to answer. Alone,
she fills in what she imagines

might be the remainder.
She assumes the pressing
question must be who is

the father of the unborn child
she carries. It's not the red-haired
painter, and that's all she'll say.

But what if the truth-loving
question turns out to be
"Who is Gordina de Groot?"

Will she speak of the potatoes
every member of her family
has a hand in raising,

saying she too was planted
in the Brabant? After that,
she muses, what more is there

to tell, as if anyone here
would listen. Long past the meal,
the full-flushed question lingers,

"Who am I first of all?"
but, frankly, can she answer
without adding "What does it matter?"

Still Lifes

Frittillaries in a Copper Vase
Painting, oil on canvas
Paris: April – May, 1887
Musée d'Orsay, Paris

STILL LIFES
Paris, March 1886 – Feb. 1888

Markets of Montmartre
and all over Paris, opulent
with buds and blossoms,
furnish me with seductive
subjects for my brushes.

I am striving to brighten
and lighten my palette,
turning away from the same
gray earth I've labored
to capture on past canvases.

I try spiky fritillaries
in a copper pot before
a peacock blue background,
or a batch of violet dahlias
against intense yellow.

The colors tremble and glow
when their opposites
mingle to *form a couple
which complete each other
like man and woman.*

What astonishes me,
when I stand back, is not
my single passion to pair colors
but their unflinching intimacy,
but how they need each other

and how that is enough.

The Blunt Grace Of Sunlight

The Sower
Painting, oil on canvas
Arles: June, 1888
Kröller-Müller Museum
The Netherlands

THE BLUNT GRACE OF SUNLIGHT
Arles, 1888 - 1889

In the history of God's silence, the sun
feeds more than pink peach trees,
lilacs, lavender, the larkspurs, and all
the toothed and lance-shaped leaves.

Even when the sun seems remote
and tired, its light can entice
timid buds out of their bunkers
in the frost-locked ground.

And after winter's crude shrapnel,
ice-blown, cold, and our clothes
layered like bandages,
how warm it feels on the flesh.

It's easy to imagine a moth
as it slips out of its sheath
of custodial skin and dances
like something set free.

The moth doesn't ask if any tactic's
better? The returning songbird
doesn't question the essential
exuberance spreading everywhere.

The weightless motion of sunlight
as it stretches, almost edgeless,
suffuses the whole moment,
alive with beginnings.

This is the unspoken agreement,
unguarded and sweet as peace,
that the sun bestows its embrace
and, in return, earth flourishes.

Something About Bridges

The Langlois Bridge at Arles
Painting, Oil on Canvas
Arles: May, 1888
Wallraf-Richartz Museum
Cologne, Germany

SOMETHING ABOUT BRIDGES

piques my curiosity. Possibly
        the way
they balance between
        opposite
embankments, straddling
        each side
so the impartial road
        presses onward
with no diversions.

For days, I devour hours
        looking at
a little drawbridge
        across
the canal's thin channel,
        whose water
glistens like blue topaz
        lit by
the sun's humble labor,

so at first I fail to catch
        the tacit
arrangement of one
        washerwoman
bowed down with work
        that frees
the genteel lady of the house
        to spend
afternoons under her parasol,
        taking
a stroll over the little bridge.

The Night Café
Painting, oil on canvas
Arles: September, 1888
Yale University Art Gallery,
New Haven, Connecticut

In Arles

The Bedroom
Painting, oil on canvas
Arles: October, 1888
Van Gogh Museum, Amsterdam

IN ARLES

Color is to do everything, Vincent said in Arles:
walls of blue violet and yellow bed in Arles.

Obsessed with citron sunflowers that turn their heads,
he paints to seize their fire before they're dead in Arles.

Outdoors, Gauguin and van Gogh, drawing side by side,
look in opposite directions instead, in Arles.

Clouded by absinthe in the hellish café light,
Vincent hurls a glass at Gauguin's head in Arles.

Alone, van Gogh paints: green chin, rust-red eye sockets,
white lips and bandaged ear. So much unsaid in Arles.

Self-Portrait with Bandaged Ear
Painting, oil on canvas
Arles: January, 1889
Courtauld Institute
Galleries, London

Rachel of Arles

Sunflowers
Painting, oil on canvas
Arles: August, 1888
National Gallery, London

RACHEL OF ARLES

                        I begin,
Vincent, to regard your closeness
in matched colors: stormy sky
blue eyes, the orange of your beard.

                 Some days you entered
full of sunflowers, those big ugly eyes
that watched while walls had ears
for the wild side.

                     Your head
not yet a hill of bandages,
you saw how Rachels often end up empty
and whispered about a wedding of two
complementary colors.

                   And I half-
hearing you rave late into night
about the fullness of color: how grays glow
with a bridelike blush and yellow in woodwork
wavers out and into shadows.

                    With your scent
of turpentine, absinthe and death, you gave me
more than I bargained for. The Christmas
you brought me the razored section
of your left ear, I turned away,
not wanting to see what wasn't there.

In the Arena

Spectators in the Arena at Arles
Oil on Canvas
Arles: December 1888
The State Hermitage Museum,
St. Petersburg, Russia

IN THE ARENA

When I gave you my earlobe as a gift,
saying, *Keep this object like a treasure,*
I was not acting like the parish priest

who places a wafer on your tongue
in memory of a sacrifice he didn't make,
but rather I was recalling bullfights

in the arena under a blazing sun
when the crowd waved their arms
and brandished hats, hollering

copious bravoes toward the matador.
Dressed in sky-blue piped in gold,
he paraded around the sandy ring,

holding up the severed ear,
before bestowing his trophy
to a tantalizing, local beauty.

Bear in mind I imagine,
more and more, I am less
the matador than the maligned

animal, baited and struck down.
Day after day, sun-wracked
and fury-faced, I am a dumb beast

who can't amend his own rage
while even the arena allows
an animal the dignity of a good fight.

Malice

Reaper with Sickle (after Millet)
Painting, Oil on Canvas
Saint- Rémy, France Sept., 1889
Amsterdam, The Netherlands

MALICE

Roving crowds of mostly youths
hound me in the streets and jeer,
or hurl rotten fruit at my head,
while eighty neighbors claim
I am a danger to myself and others.
Even the crows overhead,
those dark, accusing angels,
call down "crazed, crazed."

And the dead? They gather
in scrawny groups and gawk
with long, disdainful faces,
or counsel that the color
of an autumnal sky
cannot be named. They hiss
through their remaining teeth,
chastising, "Vincent, Vincent."

Vincent van Gogh's House (The Yellow House)
Paining, Oil on Canvas
Arles: Sept., 1888
Van Gogh Museum, Amsterdam

Van Gogh's Hats

Self-Portrait with Dark Felt Hat
Painting, oil on canvas
Paris: Spring, 1886
Van Gogh Museum,
Amsterdam

Self-Portrait with Grey Felt Hat
Painting, oil on canvas
Paris: Spring, 1886
Van Gogh Museum,
Amsterdam

VAN GOGH'S HATS
from his self-portraits

First the dark felt hat of March
of 1886. An earnest and elegant hat.
The coal-black hat of a man emerging
out of the shadows. Hat of the pensive mood
and the clean-clipped beard and mustache.
A tactful hat, a comme il faut chapeau
for afternoons at leisure in the Louvre
gazing at the Rembrandts. Hat of business
acumen; the borrowed, black homburg
that likely belonged to his brother.

Or the faint-gray hat of the winter of 1887.
Grizzled like the glow in bistros and bars
during hours drinking absinthe. Morning fog
on the river and head in the clouds slouch hat.
Transforming little dots of color into longer
dashes hat. Sleek city hat of the fleeting affair
with a café owner. Emerging damaged
crush hat. The racket and tainted air
of Paris cap. The sad hat of so many painters,
infesting like fleas. The *get up and go forth* hat.

See the straw hat on the sojourn in the South.
The *I'm up to my ears in work,* everything's
In blossom brimmed hat. An immense sea
of buttercups, clusters of sunflowers,
Wheat fields, haystacks, and always
The striving for *the high yellow note* hat.
The non-stop painting from daybreak
Until sunset straw hat with a broken brim.
The cap of intoxicating color and energy,
Hat without limits, agitated and unruly.

The ragged blue hat over the bandaged ear,
painted as if to say *I am completely recovered
And am at work again and everything is normal.*
A hat this ugly must be one saved
From the trash heap. Hat that won't hide
The anguished past. A frail hat that gives
Comfort. Hat with manic fur overflowing
In all directions across the forehead.
The darkly troubled hat, familiar fur cap
Headed to the asylum. The last hat.

Self-Portrait with Straw Hat
Painting, oil on canvas
Paris: Summer, 1887
The Detroit Institute of Art,
Detroit, Michigan

Self-Portrait with Bandaged Ear
Painting, oil on canvas
Arles: January, 1889
Courtauld Institute

Irises

Irises
Painting, oil on Canvas
Saint- Rémy, France May, 1889
Getty Center, Los Angeles, California

IRISES
St. Paul-de-Mausole Asylum
St. Rémy-de-Provence, France, May 1889

Outside the asylum, an overgrown garden
borders a courtyard where, my first week here,
I notice a surfeit of irises and set up my easel
to paint near a plain, unperturbed fountain.

From discrete distances, the other patients
watch as I work; they don't disturb me.
Later when I walk through the arched hallways
of the hospital, I hear their howls and ravings.

I think I have done well to come here as I am
starting to discard my dread. Others too
vouch they hear voices and strange sounds
during their attacks. *And that lessens the horror.*

On canvas, I paint fragile petals, lapis blues
to indigo. I try to capture each peculiar pivot
and bend of every head, even the one white
blossom almost on the edge of other frantic,
and frail, flowers.

The Death's Head Moth

Emperor Moth
Painting, oil on canvas
Saint- Rémy, France
May, 1889
Van Gogh Museum, Amsterdam

THE DEATH'S HEAD MOTH

First I heard its urgent chirping
Before I found the sound
Emerged from one enormous

Moth with winsome tints:
Cloud-white tinged with carmine,
Vaguely shading off to olive-green

After its color, I discovered
The small human skull
Emblazoned on its body

like the cinderous imprint
Priests place on foreheads
On Ash Wednesday

To prompt the prodigal sinner
And the unwavering saved
To reflect on Death.

No doubt, some suspect
that enshrouded Death
Never dressed itself

In a scrim of such
Translucent beauty
To quiver and float

In dusk's uncertain light.
But why not?
Ask the common skullcap

and the yellow-rattle
Whether there'll be trumpets
Or trilling choruses at the end.

As for me, I'm such a fool
For beauty that I want
To believe Death

Will untether me, a grub,
So I can flutter, iridescent,
In unfamiliar light.

Cypress Trees

CYPRESSES
Painting, oil on canvas
Saint-Rémy, France: June, 1889
The Metropolitan Museum of Art,
New York

CYPRESS TREES
June, 1889

Their blackness fascinates me:
    flickering, inky
to a somber bottle-green.

Against the sky's intense blue,
    these trees strive upward,
shaped like massive flames.

They tremble in gentle drafts
    but writhe, almost capsizing,
When winter's mistrals roil.

I see cypresses as sentinels,
    defiant against forces
Struggling to uproot them.

Going back to their black notes,
    I try to capture some
of their internal turbulence

with intricate crescents
    and arcs like vapors rising,
but the black remains

an impenetrable darkness,
    so close to my own grave
storms and torment.

Starry Night

Starry Night
Painting, oil on canvas
Saint—Rémy, France: June, 1889
The Museum of Modern Art, New York

STARRY NIGHT

> "I had another dream in which I saw the
> Sun, the moon, and eleven stars bowing,
> down to me." Genesis 37:9

Time after time Gauguin harangued me,
fixing his eyes on me in snickering contempt,
for not composing paintings from memory,

but my mind is an unwelcoming country
f ull of delusions and dangerous ravings.
Why should I invite enfeebling demons

to inspire me when the simple demeanor
of open countryside provides a comforting
model to color straight onto the canvas?

●

From my sleeping cell in the asylum, I look
east and southeast over a spacious landscape
and have an unhampered view of the vast

night sky. By and large, *the sight of the stars
makes me dream* while dark silhouettes
of hills repose, placid and motionless.

The cypresses striking skyward remind me
of church spires in the stern villages
and flat farmlands of my childhood

when, even then, the immense skies of night
were more alive and lushly colored than day.
Beyond the horizon, preachers said, waits paradise

But I believe night is active, pulsing with stars.
when I used to walk at night, I felt a sense of awe
envelop me I the way a hush engulfs the sleeping

towns and somehow the dark night dissolved
my painful doubts and swept away my failures.
Painting the starry sky is another way to walk at night.

•

I come to each canvas wanting to go deep within
the intricate worlds but my curious journey
seems confounded by sets of simple contrasts

—near and far, old and new, open and closed.
Contour becomes more insistent in my pieces
as if I'm trying too map an impassioned landscape

with tumultuous trees, rocks and ravines
or to chart stars sparkling within reach
of the stretching arms of spiral galaxies.

When I'm enwrapped in painting a night panorama,
for some flushed moments I feel great pleasure
as though I indeed can make trees touch the sky,

as though these stars gaze upon the lumpish earth
—and me— and nod their citron heads in approval,
blinking back astonishment at what I've made.

Painting the Stars

Starry Night over the Rhone
Painting, oil on canvas
Arles, Sept., 1888
Musée d'Orsay. Paris

PAINTING THE STARS

Painting the far-flung stars is as close to prayer
as a whore passing for an angel in dreams.
How can I say what grace such darkness will bear?

I watch the lamps of heaven waver and flare.
So out of reach, like a strumpet's esteem.
Painting the far-flung stars, I suppose, is prayer.

I guess God pierces the meniscus of air
d installs each star as a distant dot that gleams.
How can I say what grace such darkness will bear?

On earth, even dirt cradles meek seeds with care
while I hunger for more than food, it seems.
My painting the far-flung stars is close to prayer.

Alone, I feel broken in life, and often despair
of locating solace in my few earthy schemes.
How can I say what grace such darkness will bear?

Painting the far-flung stars is as close to prayer
as my constant talk of love amid tears and screams.
Lost or saved, I turn my face to the far elsewhere.
How can I say what grace such darkness will bear?

Branch of an Almond Tree in Bloom

Almond Blossom
Painting, oil on canvas
Saint-Rémy, France: February, 1890
Van Gogh Museum, Amsterdam

BRANCH OF AN ALMOND TREE IN BLOOM
February, 1890

Sometimes I wonder where are the tulips
of youth. I can recollect only a few
flowers from that time – pink hyacinths,
sweet peas, forget-me-nots and violets.
For the remainder of my life, my mind
fills in with common thistles and burdock,
wildflowers of roadsides and waste places.

But for my new nephew and namesake,
born in Paris the last day of January
when almond trees blossom in Provence,
I'm painting a canvas for his bedroom,
in hopes he'll recall gauzy, white flowers
as if lying in his cradle looking up
through flowering arms to a sublime sky.

Road with Cypress and Star

Road with Cypress and Star
Painting, oil on canvas
Saint-Rémy, France:
May 12 - 15, 1890
Kröller-Müller Museum,
Otterlo, The Netherlands

ROAD WITH CYPRESS AND STAR
one of his last paintings before leaving the asylum and Provence May 12 – 15, 1890

Not in itself
a destination,
the road goes
towards and away.
And always, each
taken step remains
end and beginning.

Night can be both
today and tomorrow,
like a snake shedding skin.
Mention the moon and
what one witnesses
is the sun's light
on its blanched face.

See the two cypresses,
side by side, flicker
as one flame —
even though the road rises
to swamp both trunks
as they surge from earth,
seeking heaven.

The spirits of the dead,
who come alive
in memories, return,
the way stars appear,
one by one,
until the sky shines
with remembered light.

At Last

Wheatfield with Crows
Painting, oil on canvas
Auvers-sur-Oise, France: July, 1890
Van Gogh Museum, Amsterdam

AT LAST
"Wheat Field with Crows"

I'm pulled back to the subdued
northern light I knew from my youth,
as if tethered to its native darkness.

I feel at home with smoky half-tones
of golds and grays of these wheat fields.
Where else could I answer the crows

darting toward me, calling down
their frantic "amaze me, amaze me"
then by putting color to the courage

of these stalks of wheat, steadfastly
rising outside of Auvers? Every day,
in my painting, I seem summoned

to something beyond my meager self.
In Auvers, at last I am free to pursue
the dark landscape itself, devoid

of distracting human encounters.
The road snaking into the wheat field,
has enough sullen hues of blood and flesh.

Among the stalks, I hear wheat whisper
its benediction as if begging me to paint
this austere place and its distraught sky.

July 1890

Wheat Fields with Auvers in the Background
Painting, oil on canvas
Auvers-sur-Oise: July, 1890
Musée d'art et d'Histoire
Geneva, Switzerland

JULY 1890

For days on end, he gave his heart
to the canvas, brushstroke
by ardent and agitated
brushstroke, while rusty fields
of wheat heaved and recoiled
around him like a tormented ocean.

Engulfed in his own sullen judgment
that everything treasured he touched
either turned rancid or vanished,

on a summer Sunday, he waded
into the wheat with his canvas
and brushes, his paints and a pistol
– which no one knew how he found –
and fired, hitting himself in the chest.
Below the heart. Another botched job.

Careful to button up his coat
to hide the blood, he staggered back,
back to the bed in his rented room,

unruffled, ready to let go,
to sink into himself,
As Death drifted toward him

A List of Van Gogh's Artwork Mentioned in these Poems

F = Jacob Baart de la Faille catalogue number
JH = Dr. Jan Hulsker catalogue number

The titles of drawings and paintings, as well as where and when they were done, and where they now reside, was taken from *The Van Gogh Gallery* on the Internet.

SELF PORTRAIT IN FRONT OF AN EASEL
Painting, Oil on Canvas
Paris, 1888
Van Gogh Museum
Amsterdam
F: 522, JH: 1356

PEASANT WITH SICKLE, SEEN FROM THE BACK
Drawing: Black chalk
Nuenen: August, 1885
Kröller-Müller Museum
Otterloo, the Netherlands
F: 1322v:, JH:865

DIGGER
Watercolor: charcoal, watercolor,
heightened with white
Etten: September, 1881
Kröller-Müller Museum, Otterlo, The Netherlands
F: 855, JH: 43

ROAD IN ETTEN
Drawing: pencil, washed
Etten: October, 1881
The Metropolitan Museum of Art, New York
F: 1678, JH: 46

SORROW
stanza 2:
"Bent Figure of a Woman (Sien?)"
Drawing: pencil, pen, brush, sepia, washed
The Hague: May - early in the month, 1882
Kröller-Müller Museum, Otterlo, The Netherlands
F: 935, JH: 143

Stanza 3:
"Bent Figure of a Woman"
Drawing: pencil, pen, brush, sepia, washed
The Hague: May - early in the month, 1882
Kröller-Müller Museum, Otterlo, The Netherlands
F: 937, JH: 144

stanza 6:
"Sien with Cigar Sitting on the Floor near Stove"
Drawing: pencil, black chalk, pen, brush, sepia, heightened with white
The Hague: April – late in month, 1882
Kröller-Müller Museum, Otterlo, The Netherlands
F: 898, JH: 141

stanzas 8 and 9:
"Sorrow"
Drawing, black chalk
The Hague: April 10, 1882
Walshall Museum and Art Gallery, Walshall, UK
F: 929a, JH: 130

ARTIST'S SIGNATURE
"A Pair of Boots"
Painting, oil on canvas
Paris: early year, 1887
The Baltimore Museum of Art, The Cone Collection
Baltimore, Maryland
F:333, JH: 1236

GORDINA DE GROOT
"The Potato Eaters"
Painting, oil on canvas
Nuenen, The Netherlands: April, 1885
Van Gogh Museum, Amsterdam
F: 82, JH: 764

STILL LIFES
stanza 3:
"Frittillaries in a Copper Vase"
Painting, oil on canvas
Paris: April – May, 1887
Musée d'Orsay, Paris
F: 213, JH: 1247

THE BLUNT GRACE OF SUNSHINE
" The Sower"
Painting, oil on canvas
Arles: June, 1888
Kröller-Müller Museum
Otterloo, The Netherlands
F: 422, JH:1470

SOMETHING ABOUT BRIDGES
"The Langlois Bridge at Arles"
Painting, oil on canvas
Arles: May, 1888
Wallraf-Richartz-Museum
Cologne, Germany
F: 570, JH: 1421

IN ARLES
stanza 1:
"The Bedroom"
Painting, oil on canvas
Arles: October, 1888
Van Gogh Museum, Amsterdam
F: 482, JH: 1608

stanza 4:
"The Night Café "
Painting, oil on canvas
Arles: September, 1888
Yale University Art Gallery, New Haven, Connecticut:
F:463, JH:1575

Stanza 5:
"Self Portrait with Bandaged Ear"
Painting, oil on canvas
Arles: January, 1889
Courtauld Institute Galleries, London
F:527, JH:1657

RACHEL OF ARLES
"Sunflowers"
Painting, oil on canvas
Arles: August, 1888
National Gallery, London
F: 454, JH: 1562

IN THE ARENA
"Spectators in the Arena at Arles"
Painting, oil on canvas
Arles: December, 1888
Hermitage, St. Petersburg, Russia
F: 548, JH: 1653

MALICE
Stanza 1: Reaper with Sickle (after Millet)"
Painting, oil on canvas
St-Rémy, Sept., 1889
Van Gogh Museum, Amsterdam
F:687, JH1782

"Vincent Van Gogh's House"
(The Yellow House)
Painting, oil on canvas
Arles, September 1888
Van Gogh Museum, Amsterdam
F:464 JH:1563

VAN GOGH'S HATS
stanza 1:
"Self-Portrait with Dark Felt Hat"
Painting, oil on canvas
Paris: Spring, 1886
Van Gogh Museum, Amsterdam
F: 208a, JH: 1089

VAN GOGH'S HATS
stanza 2:
"Self-Portrait with Grey Felt Hat"
Painting, oil on canvas
Paris: March – April, 1887

stanza 3:
"Self-Portrait with Straw Hat"
Painting, oil on canvas
Paris: Summer, 1887
The Detroit Institute of Art, Detroit, Michigan
F: 526, JH: 1309

stanza 4:
"Self-Portrait with Bandaged Ear"
see above
F: 527, JH: 1657

IRISES
"Irises"
Painting, oil on canvas
Saint-Rémy, France: May, 1889
Getty Center, Los Angeles, California
F: 608, JH: 1691

THE DEATH'S HEAD MOTH
"Emperor Moth"
Painting, oil on canvas
Saint-Rémy, France: May, 1889
Van Gogh Museum, Amsterdam
F: 610, JH: 1702

CYPRESS TREES
"Cypresses"
Painting, oil on canvas
Saint-Rémy, France: June, 1889
The Metropolitan Museum of Art, New York
F: 613, JH: 1746

STARRY NIGHT
"Starry Night"
Painting, oil on canvas
Saint-Rémy, France: June, 1889
The Museum of Modern Art, New York
F: 612, JH: 1731

PAINTING THE STARS
"Starry Night over the Rhone"
Painting, oil on canvas
Arles: Sept., 1888
Musée d'Orsay
Paris, France
F: 474, JH: 1592

BRANCH OF AN ALMOND TREE IN BLOOM
"Almond Blossom"
Painting, oil on canvas
Saint-Rémy, France: February, 1890
Van Gogh Museum, Amsterdam
F: 671, JH: 1891

ROAD WITH CYPRESS AND STAR
"Road with Cypress and Star"
Painting, oil on canvas
Saint-Rémy, France: May 12 - 15, 1890
Kröller-Müller Museum, Otterlo, The Netherlands
F: 683, JH: 1982

AT LAST
"Wheatfield with Crows"
Painting, oil on canvas
Auvers-sur-Oise, France: July, 1890
Van Gogh Museum, Amsterdam
F: 779, JH: 2117

JULY 1890
"Wheat Fields with Auvers in the Background"
Painting, oil on canvas
Auvers-sur-Oise: July, 1890
Musée d'Art et d'Histoire
Geneva, Switzerland
F: 801, JH: 2123

www.ingramcontent.com/pod-product-compliance
Lightning Source LLC
Chambersburg PA
CBHW042305150426
43197CB00001B/16